11+
PRACTICE PAPERS
BOOK 3

Series editor Tracey Phelps, the 11+ tutor with a

96% PASS RATE

Maths

T0382087

English

Verbal Reasoning

Non-verbal Reasoning

Ages 10–11

est

SCHOLASTIC

Published in the UK by Scholastic, 2021

Book End, Range Road, Witney, Oxfordshire, OX29 0YD

Scholastic Ireland, 89E Lagan Road, Dublin Industrial Estate,
Glasnevin, Dublin, D11 HP5F

www.scholastic.co.uk

© 2021 Scholastic Limited

1 2 3 4 5 6 7 8 9   1 2 3 4 5 6 7 8 9 0

A CIP catalogue record for this book is available from the
British Library.

ISBN 978-1407-19080-8

Printed and bound by Ashford Colour Press Ltd
Paper made from wood grown in sustainable forests and
other controlled sources.

Author
Tracey Phelps

Editorial team
Rachel Morgan, Vicki Yates,Sarah Davies, Julia Roberts

Design team
Dipa Mistry, Andrea Lewis and and Couper Street Type Co

Illustration
Tracey Phelps

Contents

About the CEM test and this book

About the CEM test

The Centre for Evaluation and Monitoring (CEM) is one of the leading providers of the tests that grammar schools use in selecting students at 11+. The CEM test assesses a student's ability in Verbal Reasoning, Non-verbal Reasoning, English and Mathematics. Pupils typically take the CEM test at the start of Year 6.

Students answer multiple-choice questions and record their answers on a separate answer sheet. This answer sheet is then marked via OMR (Optical Mark Recognition) scanning technology.

The content and question type may vary slightly each year. The English and Verbal Reasoning components have included synonyms, antonyms, word associations, shuffled sentences, cloze (gap-fill) passages and comprehension questions.

The Mathematics and Non-verbal Reasoning components span the Key Stage 2 Mathematics curriculum, with emphasis on worded problems. It is useful to note that the CEM test may include Mathematics topics that students will be introduced to in Year 6, such as ratio, proportion and probability.

The other main provider of such tests is GL Assessment. The GLA test assesses the same subjects as the CEM test and uses a multiple-choice format.

About this book

Scholastic 11+ Practice Papers for the CEM Test Ages 10–11 Book 3 is part of the Pass Your 11+ series. The practice papers in this book have been designed to accurately reflect the format and style of the CEM test. The CEM test consists of two question papers, each of which contains elements of the four subjects being tested. Each test paper is divided into four or five sections, with strict timings for each section. Students are not permitted to move backwards or forwards between the different sections during the test.

This book offers:

- Two full-length CEM-style papers to familiarise your child with the CEM test.
- Timings for each section to help your child become accustomed to working under time pressure.
- Multiple-choice questions to practise answering the types of question your child will meet in their CEM test.
- Multiple-choice answer sheets.
- Answers.
- Visit **https://shop.scholastic.co.uk/pass-your-11-plus/extras** for a copy of the extended answers and additional answer sheets. This information can also be accessed via the QR code opposite.

CEM-style 11+ Mixed Assessment Practice Paper A

Information about this practice paper:

- The time allowed is given at the start of each section.

- The page number appears at the bottom of each page.

- The title of each section is provided at the start of each section.

- Use the pages of the test to write your workings out.

- Answers should be clearly marked in pencil on the answer sheets on pages 34 and 35, in the spaces provided. Additional answer sheets are available at **https://shop.scholastic.co.uk/pass-your-11-plus/extras**.

- If you make a mistake, rub it out and insert your new answer.

- If you are not sure of an answer, choose the one you think would be best; do not leave it blank.

 You will see this symbol at the beginning of each section. It will tell you how many minutes are allowed for that section.

Synonyms

Instructions

Select the word that has the SAME or SIMILAR meaning to the word on the left.
Mark your answer on the answer sheet (page 34) by choosing one of the options A to E.
There is only one right answer for each question.

Example 1

	A	B	C	D	E
start	end	begin	progress	least	last

The correct answer is:

B

begin

The answer, B, has been marked for you on the answer sheet.

Example 2

	A	B	C	D	E
cry	sad	tears	swear	hankie	sob

The correct answer is:

E

sob

Mark the box with the letter E on the answer sheet.

 You have **5** minutes for this section.

1		A	B	C	D	E
disclose		illustrate	suggest	uncover	indicate	concede

2		A	B	C	D	E
engaging		captivating	suspicious	gracious	inviting	refreshing

3		A	B	C	D	E
awkward		flimsy	theatrical	grouchy	artificial	clumsy

4		A	B	C	D	E
hasten		bound	hurry	spring	advance	proceed

5		A	B	C	D	E
economise		squander	trade	exchange	deal	save

6		A	B	C	D	E
fearless		adamant	resolute	enterprising	dauntless	obstinate

7		A	B	C	D	E
endless		enduring	indefinite	restricted	lengthy	boundless

8		**A**	**B**	**C**	**D**	**E**
tweak		flick	crush	shock	twitch	adjust

9		**A**	**B**	**C**	**D**	**E**
habit		custom	rule	adage	edict	order

10		**A**	**B**	**C**	**D**	**E**
steadfast		quiet	quick	firm	nice	fair

11		**A**	**B**	**C**	**D**	**E**
argument		opinion	notion	mood	quarrel	bias

12		**A**	**B**	**C**	**D**	**E**
dupe		urge	mystify	trick	juggle	entice

13		**A**	**B**	**C**	**D**	**E**
quota		fee	price	stake	share	piece

14		**A**	**B**	**C**	**D**	**E**
regenerate		refresh	recall	renew	reflect	relegate

15		A	B	C	D	E
evolve		deviate	demote	develop	defy	devise

16		A	B	C	D	E
competence		kindness	strength	scope	ability	virtue

17		A	B	C	D	E
imperil		abandon	endanger	embarrass	explode	encounter

18		A	B	C	D	E
remorseful		resentful	boastful	regretful	respectful	restful

19		A	B	C	D	E
outcome		choice	exit	vote	option	result

20		A	B	C	D	E
faithful		loyal	fitting	formal	fleeting	official

21		A	B	C	D	E
announce		delude	declare	depict	deplore	detract

22		A	B	C	D	E
ideal		feasible	clear	perfect	ready	timely

23		A	B	C	D	E
courteous		generous	odious	contrite	polite	erudite

24		A	B	C	D	E
prolong		prosper	lengthen	continue	expedite	promote

25		A	B	C	D	E
glance		gaze	glimpse	glare	stare	gloat

26		A	B	C	D	E
appear		impress	inspire	affect	seem	involve

27		A	B	C	D	E
jeer		jive	cheer	jump	jest	taunt

Comprehension

Instructions

Carefully read through the passage of writing, then answer the questions that follow.
Mark your answer on the answer sheet (page 34) by choosing one of the options A to D.
Look at the examples below.

Example passage

The boys went fishing by the river. They only caught one fish.

Example 1

Where did the boys go fishing?

A. By the river

B. In the pond

C. In the sea

D. By the lake

The correct answer is A: By the river

Find example 1 in the 'Comprehension' section on the answer sheet.

The answer, A, has been marked for you.

Example 2

How many fish did they catch?

A. Fifteen

B. None

C. Plenty

D. One

The correct answer is D: One

Mark the box with the letter D on the answer sheet for example 2.

 You have **14** minutes for this section.

Sam Cooke

Sam Cooke was born on 22 January 1931 in Clarksdale, Mississippi. He is widely credited with inventing soul music, and he contributed to the rise of legendary singers Aretha Franklin and Marvin Gaye. While he is best known for his impact on music with his distinctive voice, he is also acknowledged for his role as a major activist within the Civil Rights Movement.

5   Sam was the fifth of eight children and began singing, when aged six, in a group alongside his siblings. Throughout his teenage years and young adulthood, he performed with several gospel groups but quickly realised that he wanted to pursue a solo career. Up until this point, he had been known as Sam Cook but he added the 'e' to signify a fresh start. He broke the status quo by moving away from gospel and recording a mix of soul, and rhythm and blues. Unhappy with his deal with RCA Records,
10   Cooke established his own publishing company where he could maintain control over his music and, to retain control of his earnings, he formed his own record company. This meant that he was able to own songwriting and publishing rights over his music. He was the first black recording artist to have ultimate control over his business affairs. Cooke achieved around 30 Top 40 chart hits in less than ten years; composing the music and writing the lyrics for almost all of the songs that he recorded. He was a
15   prolific songwriter and his lyrics were poetic but could also be incredibly inspirational. In 1963, Cooke was moved upon hearing Bob Dylan's 'Blowin' in the Wind' and, ashamed that he hadn't written such a poignant anti-racism song himself, he embarked on the task of penning his own. Drawing on his own experiences, Cooke released 'A Change Is Gonna Come' in 1964. The song was influenced by the refusal to admit Cooke and his fellow singers to a Louisiana motel on the basis that it was a 'whites-
20   only' establishment. This song quickly became an anthem of the Civil Rights Movement and would have been a significant milestone in Cooke's career had it not been somewhat overshadowed by The Beatles' high-profile appearance on an American television show around the same time.

Cooke married his first wife, Dolores, in 1953 and they divorced five years later. In 1959, he insisted that he cover the cost of his ex-wife's funeral after she was killed in a tragic road traffic accident. In
25   the same year as his divorce, he married his second wife, Barbara. They had three children together but tragedy struck when their youngest, Vincent, died as a result of drowning in the family swimming pool. On 11 December 1964, Cooke was gunned down and killed in a Californian motel. The motel manager, Bertha Franklin, claimed that she fired the fatal gunshots at him in self defence, and the courts ruled the death to be a justifiable homicide. However, many have since speculated
30   and questioned the verdict. In American soul singer Etta James' book, she describes the condition of Cooke's body and highlights the fact that his injuries did not coincide with Franklin's description of the events that allegedly took place. Some believe that Cooke may have been targeted as he was considered to be an important figure in the Civil Rights Movement, often appearing alongside the likes of Malcolm X and Muhammad Ali.

35   The only concert that Cooke is reported to have ever cancelled was one that was due to take place in Memphis, Tennessee. Ahead of the show, he received a telegram notifying him that the concert that night would be segregated. Black people would make up only a quarter of the audience. None would be on the floor level and only one side of three balconies had been reserved for black audience members. When this information was confirmed to be true, he cancelled the appearance immediately and
40   released a powerful statement, emphasising his refusal to perform for a forced, segregated audience. He wanted to perform for everyone, irrespective of their ethnicity, and for his audiences to enjoy his music alongside one another. This sense of integrity meant that his was one of the first real efforts in civil disobedience that would send a message of protest in aid of the Civil Rights Movement.

1 Which of the following statements is <u>not</u> true?

A. Cooke was an inspiration, sending a clear message in support of the Civil Rights Movement.

B. Cooke was the first black performer to own the rights to his own music and recordings.

C. Cooke is the main reason that Marvin Gaye and Aretha Franklin became legends.

D. Cooke's songs sent a strong message about racial inequality.

---

2 In what year did Sam Cooke marry his second wife?

A. 1958

B. 1953

C. 1959

D. 1957

---

3 '...he hadn't written such a poignant anti-racism song himself...' (lines 16 and 17)

What does the word 'poignant' mean in this context?

A. angry

B. progressive

C. honest

D. touching

---

4 In which American state was Cooke killed?

A. Louisiana

B. California

C. Tennessee

D. Mississippi

5   Why wasn't the release of 'A Change Is Gonna Come' more of a career milestone for Cooke?

A. People deemed it to be too reformist.

B. People were too distracted by the news of Cooke's death.

C. 'Blowin' in the Wind' had already been released, so it wasn't original.

D. It was overlooked as The Beatles made a television appearance around the same time.

---

6   How many Top 40 chart hits did Cooke have?

A. Ten

B. Fewer than ten

C. Approximately 30

D. Around 50

---

7   When Cooke started his solo career, what genres of music did he mix?

A. Gospel and soul

B. Jazz and soul

C. Rhythm and blues, and gospel

D. Soul, and rhythm and blues

---

8   What age was Cooke when he was killed?

A. 33 years, 11 months and 19 days

B. 33 years, 10 months and 19 days

C. 33 years, 10 months and 21 days

D. 33 years, 11 months and 21 days

9 '...emphasising his refusal to perform for a forced, segregated audience' (line 40)

What is meant here by 'forced, segregated audience'?

A. The audience would have been forced to mix with strangers.

B. The audience would have been separated by race.

C. The audience would have been organised by height.

D. The audience would have been forced to remain seated.

_____

10 Who wrote a song that made Cooke feel ashamed that he himself hadn't written a song like it before?

A. Muhammad Ali

B. Etta James

C. Marvin Gaye

D. Bob Dylan

_____

11 'He was a prolific songwriter...' (lines 14 and 15)

Which of the following is a synonym for 'prolific'?

A. perfect

B. productive

C. prominent

D. political

_____

12 Why did Cooke add the 'e' to the end of his surname?

A. To mark the beginning of a fresh start

B. To separate himself from his siblings

C. To annoy everyone who advised him otherwise

D. To break the status quo

13 Which two events occurred in 1964?

A. Cooke's death and the release of 'A Change Is Gonna Come'

B. The birth of Cooke's eldest child and Cooke's death

C. The release of 'A Change Is Gonna Come' and the death of Cooke's first wife, Dolores

D. The release of 'A Change Is Gonna Come' and Cooke establishing his own record company

14 Which part of the Tennessee venue was reserved for black people?

A. The floor level

B. The three balcony levels

C. One side of the third balcony level

D. One side of three balconies

15 Why did Etta James doubt the court's verdict?

A. She believed he was killed as a result of his links to the Civil Rights Movement.

B. The injuries sustained did not match Franklin's statement.

C. Cooke had appeared with Malcolm X and Muhammad Ali a lot.

D. She had a gut feeling.

16 How old was Cooke when he started singing in an ensemble with his siblings?

A. Five years old

B. Eight years old

C. Six years old

D. Nine years old

17 What was the significance of Cooke refusing to perform for a segregated audience?

A. It wasn't significant.

B. It was the first time anyone had spoken out against segregation.

C. Until then, Cooke had not publicised his support of the Civil Rights Movement.

D. It was among the first examples of civil disobedience, promoting the Civil Rights Movement.

18 Why did Cooke start his own record and publishing companies?

A. He wasn't happy with the deal he had with RCA Records.

B. He felt RCA Records weren't the right fit for him.

C. RCA Records were prejudiced.

D. RCA Records weren't ethically aligned with him.

19 What did 'A Change Is Gonna Come' become?

A. A football chant

B. A state song

C. An anthem of the Civil Rights Movement

D. A rock anthem

20 Which of the following is not a reason why Cooke had become an important figure in the Civil Rights Movement?

A. He wrote a poignant anti-racism song.

B. He spoke out and stood his ground about racial inequality.

C. He appeared alongside the likes of Malcolm X and Muhammad Ali.

D. He marched with Martin Luther King Jr.

Instructions

There is a set of pictures on the left with a missing picture shown by a question mark.
Pick one of the pictures from the right to complete the set. Choose one of the options A to E.

Example 1

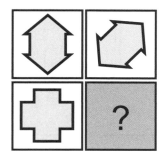 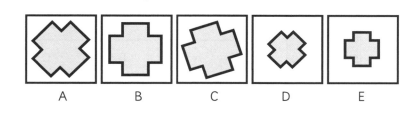

The answer to example 1 is A.

The answer, A, has been marked for you on the answer sheet (page 34).

Example 2

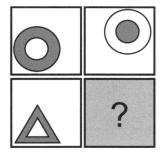 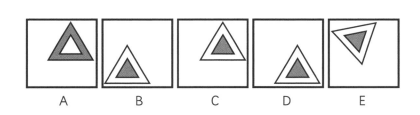

The answer to example 2 is C.

Mark the box with the letter C on the answer sheet.

 You have 9 minutes for this section.

1

A   B   C   D   E

2

A   B   C   D   E

3

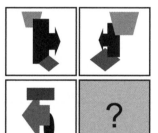

A   B   C   D   E

4

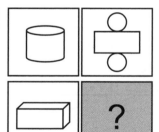

    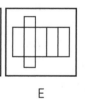

A   B   C   D   E

5

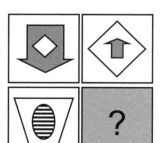

A   B   C   D   E

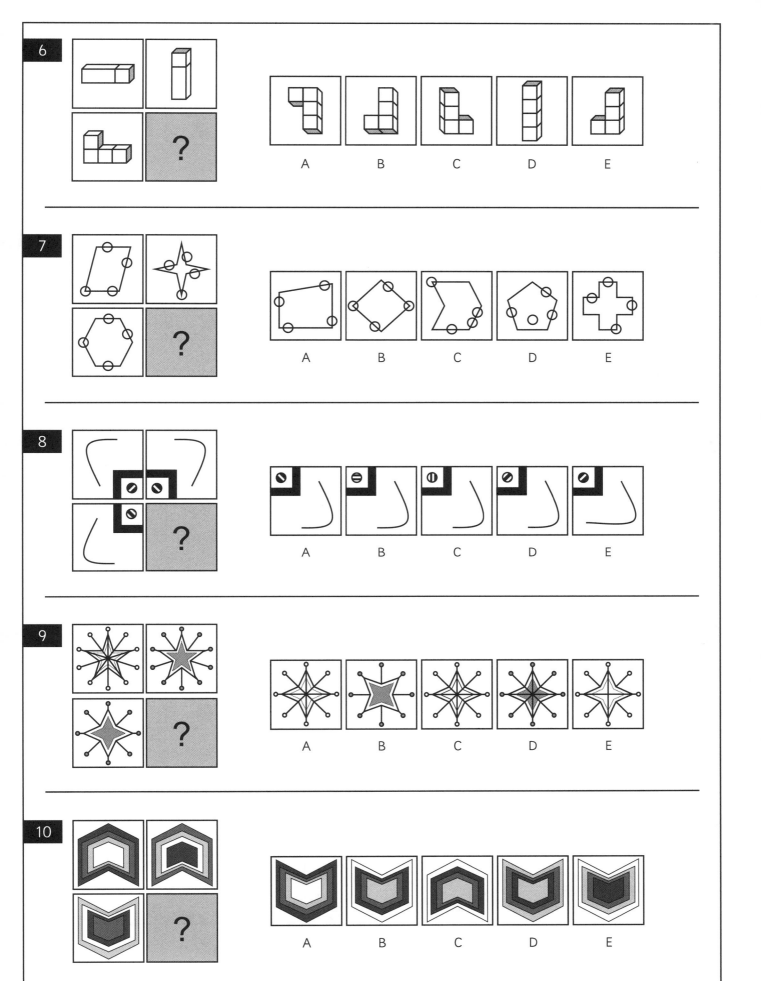

11

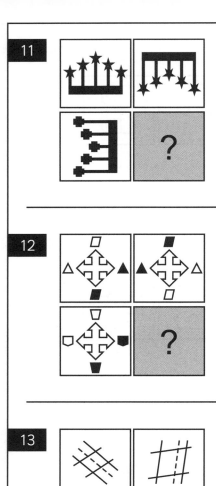

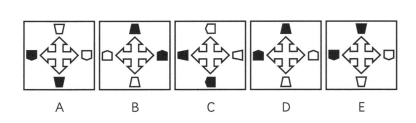

A   B   C   D   E

12

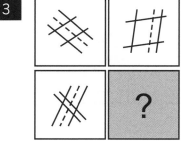

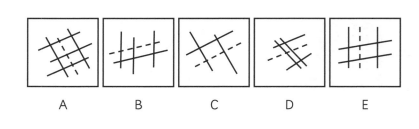

A   B   C   D   E

13

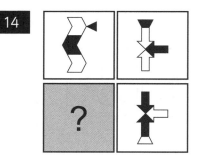

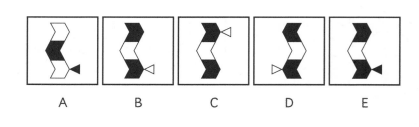

A   B   C   D   E

14

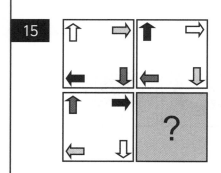

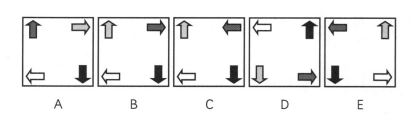

A   B   C   D   E

15

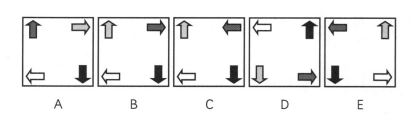

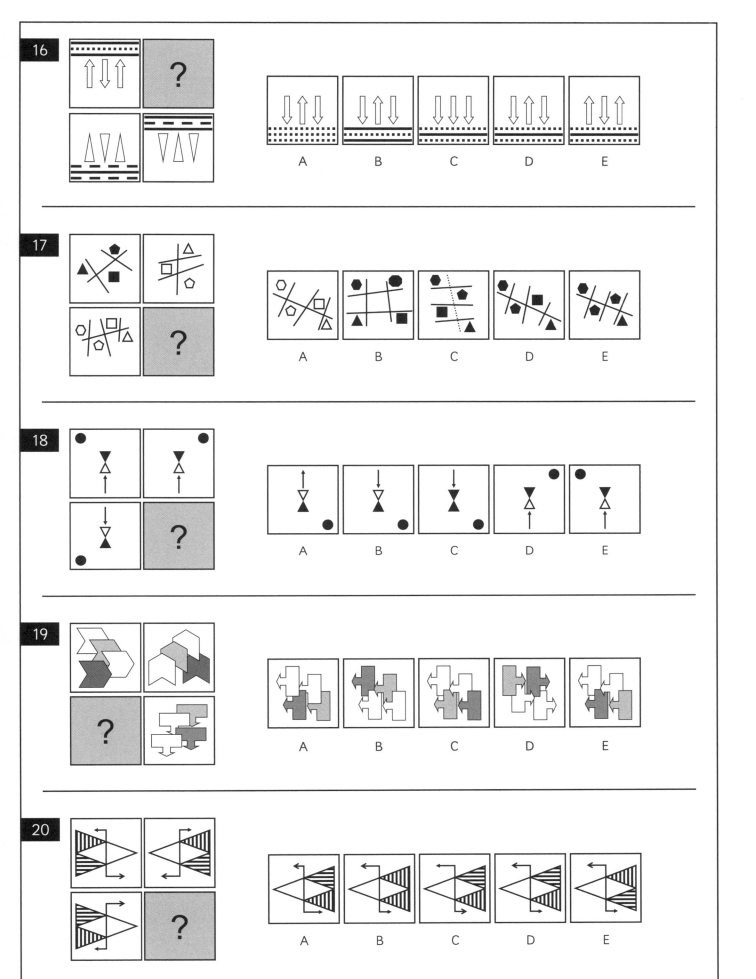

Maths 1

Instructions

In this section, choose one option from A to E to answer the question. Mark your answer on the answer sheet (page 35) by choosing one of the options A to E. Look at the examples below.

Example 1

What is 14 + 38?

A	B	C	D	E
54	52	62	64	48

The answer is:

B
52

The answer, B, has been marked for you on the answer sheet.

Example 2

Which of the following numbers is a squared number greater than 64 and smaller than 100?

A	B	C	D	E
121	49	144	81	100

The answer is:

D
81

Mark the box with the letter D on the answer sheet.

 You have 12 minutes for this section.

1 What fraction of a day is 14 hours?

A	B	C	D	E
$\frac{5}{12}$	$\frac{7}{12}$	$\frac{1}{2}$	$\frac{3}{4}$	$\frac{2}{7}$

2 Jules is stacking building bricks of height 3cm next to a different stack of bricks of height 4cm, alongside a third stack of bricks measuring 5cm in height.

What is the lowest height at which the three stacks are at the same height?

A	B	C	D	E
30cm	28cm	56cm	72cm	60cm

3 A train takes 1 hour and 5 minutes to travel between Bristol and Oxford. Mabel starts the journey in Bristol at 10.05am. The train is able to travel faster than expected and arrives in Oxford a quarter of an hour early.

At what time does Mabel reach her destination?

A	B	C	D	E
11.05am	11.10am	10.50am	10.55am	11.00am

4 What is the square root of 169?

A	B	C	D	E
14	12.5	13	15	12

5 Which two numbers have a sum of 25 and a product of 156?

A	B	C	D	E
13 and 12	10 and 15	11 and 14	9 and 16	8 and 17

6 Thuva is training for a September marathon event. He starts training in April and runs for 3km per day. In May he runs 4.5km each day and in June he runs 6km every day.

If this pattern continues, how many km will he run each day in August?

A	B	C	D	E
8.5km	7.5km	10.5km	9.5km	9km

7 What percentage of 60 is 24?

A	B	C	D	E
30%	35%	24%	40%	45%

8 The Nash family are flying to Dubai for a holiday. Tickets cost £760.00 each for Mr and Mrs Nash and the two children's tickets are each 25% cheaper.

What will be the total cost for the flights?

A	B	C	D	E
£2660.00	£1900.00	£2240.00	£2760.00	£1330.00

9 Which of the following numbers is both a square and a cube number?

A	B	C	D	E
36	125	64	49	8

10 How many lines of symmetry does a regular octagon have?

A	B	C	D	E
8	4	2	16	6

11 Rishita buys a new bag that has already had the price reduced by one-third.

She pays £24.00 for the bag.

What was the price of the bag before the discount was applied?

A	B	C	D	E
£34.00	£36.00	£32.50	£35.00	£33.00

12 Find the missing number.

$8 \times 6 + 6 = 9 \times 3 + ?$

A	B	C	D	E
17	69	27	37	23

13 162 cupcakes are shared among Years 3, 4 and 5 in the ratio 2:3:4.

How many cupcakes will Year 5 have?

A	B	C	D	E
36	63	81	75	72

14 Marc and Dan's ages add up to 73. Marc is seven years older than Dan.

How old is Marc?

A	B	C	D	E
40	37	41	33	38

15 Two families go for a meal in the same restaurant.

The Nair family have three portions of spaghetti bolognese and one Hawaiian pizza; they spend £29.00.

The Stewart family have two Hawaiian pizzas and three servings of spaghetti bolognese and their bill comes to a total of £39.50.

How much do the pizzas cost each?

A	B	C	D	E
£11.75	£10.50	£11.50	£12.95	£10.99

16 What is 18,422 rounded to the nearest 100?

A	B	C	D	E
18,000	18,430	19,000	18,500	18,400

17 Mrs Nowak buys four items of clothing to take on holiday.

The items cost £11.99, £3.99, £7.99 and £8.99.

How much change will Mrs Nowak receive if she pays with two £20 notes?

A	B	C	D	E
£8.02	£7.43	£7.04	£6.07	£6.86

18 Simon's watch is faulty and loses 20 seconds every hour. If he sets his watch to the correct time at exactly 08.00, what time will his watch show at 17.00?

A	B	C	D	E
16.53	16.57	17.03	17.05	16.55

19 If eight cereal bars cost £3.20, how much would ten cost?

A	B	C	D	E
£4.80	£3.60	£3.80	£4.00	£4.50

20 What is 4^2 plus 7^2?

A	B	C	D	E
65	75	78	72	69

21 What is $\frac{5}{8}$ of 300ml?

A	B	C	D	E
175ml	195ml	180ml	172ml	187.5ml

Maths 2

Instructions

In this section, mark your answer on the answer sheet (page 35) by filling in the correct number. Look at the examples below.

Example 1

What is 18 minus 12?

The answer is 6 and has been marked for you on the answer sheet.

The number 6 is written as '06' in the top boxes and the corresponding

digits '0' and '6' are marked in the boxes below.

0	6
[-0-]	[0]
[1]	[1]
[2]	[2]
[3]	[3]
[4]	[4]
[5]	[5]
[6]	[-6-]
[7]	[7]
[8]	[8]
[9]	[9]

Example 2

What is 18 × 4?

The answer is 72.

Mark the correct answer, 72, on the answer sheet.

 You have **10** minutes for this section.

1 A cafe can accommodate a maximum of 30 customers when all the tables are full.

Four of the tables can seat four customers and the rest of the tables seat two customers.

How many tables seat two people?

2 Eva's school buys 21 packs of maths textbooks.

Each pack contains six textbooks.

Unfortunately, rainwater has got into 50% of the books and they have to be returned.

How many books does the school return?

3 In a class of 32 children, 12 prefer to play netball and 14 prefer to play football.

The rest of the children like to play tennis.

How many children like to play tennis?

4 There are four people in the Premkumar family, and their mean age is 27.

Mr Premkumar is 44, Mrs Premkumar is 42 and their eldest son, Mahin, is 12.

How old is their younger son, Aayan?

5 A shop sells packs of identical batteries in packs of two, four and eight.

Anya buys four packs of eight batteries and twelve packs of four batteries.

How many more packs of four batteries must she buy if she needs a total of 100 batteries?

---

6 Farmer Emma owns a farm with 180 livestock.

She has numerous cows and pigs and one bull.

She owns 45 more pigs than cows.

How many cows does Farmer Emma own?

---

7 $\frac{2}{9}$ of a crate of bananas have to be thrown away as they have gone off.

There are 360 bananas in the crate.

How many bananas have to be discarded?

---

8 Priya is tiling her kitchen floor.

Her square tiles have sides measuring 50cm.

Her kitchen floor measures 2m by 3m.

How many tiles will Priya need to cover the entire surface of the floor?

9 Bianca has a number of books in her bag.

She has more than 12 and fewer than 20 books.

If she puts the books into sets of two, she has one book left over.

If she puts the books into sets of three, she has two books left over.

How many books does Bianca have in her bag?

---

10 Dev uses six pineapples to make 800 millilitres of pineapple juice.

How many pineapples does he need if he wants to make four litres of pineapple juice?

---

11 Lottie's granny is knitting her a new jumper.

The balls of wool that she is using are 75 metres long.

She will need a total of 525 metres of wool to complete the jumper.

How many balls of wool will Granny need?

---

12 A recipe for pancakes calls for one tablespoon of sugar to every three tablespoons of flour.

Kieran uses 20 tablespoons altogether for the mixture.

How many tablespoons of flour does he use?

Answer sheets

Student name:

Synonyms p.7

Examples:

1 [A] [B] [C] [D] [E]
2 [A] [B] [C] [D] [E]

Questions

1 [A] [B] [C] [D] [E]
2 [A] [B] [C] [D] [E]
3 [A] [B] [C] [D] [E]
4 [A] [B] [C] [D] [E]
5 [A] [B] [C] [D] [E]
6 [A] [B] [C] [D] [E]
7 [A] [B] [C] [D] [E]
8 [A] [B] [C] [D] [E]
9 [A] [B] [C] [D] [E]
10 [A] [B] [C] [D] [E]
11 [A] [B] [C] [D] [E]
12 [A] [B] [C] [D] [E]
13 [A] [B] [C] [D] [E]
14 [A] [B] [C] [D] [E]
15 [A] [B] [C] [D] [E]
16 [A] [B] [C] [D] [E]
17 [A] [B] [C] [D] [E]
18 [A] [B] [C] [D] [E]
19 [A] [B] [C] [D] [E]
20 [A] [B] [C] [D] [E]
21 [A] [B] [C] [D] [E]
22 [A] [B] [C] [D] [E]
23 [A] [B] [C] [D] [E]
24 [A] [B] [C] [D] [E]
25 [A] [B] [C] [D] [E]
26 [A] [B] [C] [D] [E]
27 [A] [B] [C] [D] [E]

Comprehension p.12

Examples:

1 [A] [B] [C] [D]
2 [A] [B] [C] [D]

Questions

1 [A] [B] [C] [D]
2 [A] [B] [C] [D]
3 [A] [B] [C] [D]
4 [A] [B] [C] [D]
5 [A] [B] [C] [D]
6 [A] [B] [C] [D]
7 [A] [B] [C] [D]
8 [A] [B] [C] [D]
9 [A] [B] [C] [D]
10 [A] [B] [C] [D]
11 [A] [B] [C] [D]
12 [A] [B] [C] [D]
13 [A] [B] [C] [D]
14 [A] [B] [C] [D]
15 [A] [B] [C] [D]
16 [A] [B] [C] [D]
17 [A] [B] [C] [D]
18 [A] [B] [C] [D]
19 [A] [B] [C] [D]
20 [A] [B] [C] [D]

Pictures 1 p.19

Examples:

1 [A] [B] [C] [D] [E]
2 [A] [B] [C] [D] [E]

Questions

1 [A] [B] [C] [D] [E]
2 [A] [B] [C] [D] [E]
3 [A] [B] [C] [D] [E]
4 [A] [B] [C] [D] [E]
5 [A] [B] [C] [D] [E]
6 [A] [B] [C] [D] [E]
7 [A] [B] [C] [D] [E]
8 [A] [B] [C] [D] [E]
9 [A] [B] [C] [D] [E]
10 [A] [B] [C] [D] [E]
11 [A] [B] [C] [D] [E]
12 [A] [B] [C] [D] [E]
13 [A] [B] [C] [D] [E]
14 [A] [B] [C] [D] [E]
15 [A] [B] [C] [D] [E]
16 [A] [B] [C] [D] [E]
17 [A] [B] [C] [D] [E]
18 [A] [B] [C] [D] [E]
19 [A] [B] [C] [D] [E]
20 [A] [B] [C] [D] [E]

Maths 1 p.24

Examples:

1	[A]	~~[B]~~	[C]	[D]	[E]
2	[A]	[B]	[C]	[D]	[E]

Questions

1	[A]	[B]	[C]	[D]	[E]
2	[A]	[B]	[C]	[D]	[E]
3	[A]	[B]	[C]	[D]	[E]
4	[A]	[B]	[C]	[D]	[E]
5	[A]	[B]	[C]	[D]	[E]
6	[A]	[B]	[C]	[D]	[E]
7	[A]	[B]	[C]	[D]	[E]
8	[A]	[B]	[C]	[D]	[E]
9	[A]	[B]	[C]	[D]	[E]
10	[A]	[B]	[C]	[D]	[E]
11	[A]	[B]	[C]	[D]	[E]
12	[A]	[B]	[C]	[D]	[E]
13	[A]	[B]	[C]	[D]	[E]
14	[A]	[B]	[C]	[D]	[E]
15	[A]	[B]	[C]	[D]	[E]
16	[A]	[B]	[C]	[D]	[E]
17	[A]	[B]	[C]	[D]	[E]
18	[A]	[B]	[C]	[D]	[E]
19	[A]	[B]	[C]	[D]	[E]
20	[A]	[B]	[C]	[D]	[E]
21	[A]	[B]	[C]	[D]	[E]

Maths 2 p.30

Examples:

1

O	6
~~[0]~~	[0]
[1]	[1]
[2]	[2]
[3]	[3]
[4]	[4]
[5]	[5]
[6]	~~[6]~~
[7]	[7]
[8]	[8]
[9]	[9]

2

[0]	[0]
[1]	[1]
[2]	[2]
[3]	[3]
[4]	[4]
[5]	[5]
[6]	[6]
[7]	[7]
[8]	[8]
[9]	[9]

Questions

Each of questions 1–12 has a two-column grid with rows [0] through [9].

1, 4, 7, 10, 2, 5, 8, 11, 3, 6, 9, 12

[0]	[0]
[1]	[1]
[2]	[2]
[3]	[3]
[4]	[4]
[5]	[5]
[6]	[6]
[7]	[7]
[8]	[8]
[9]	[9]

Answers

Synonyms
p.7

1	C
2	A
3	E
4	B
5	E
6	D
7	E
8	E
9	A
10	C
11	D
12	C
13	D
14	C
15	C
16	D
17	B
18	C
19	E
20	A
21	B
22	C
23	D
24	B
25	B
26	D
27	E

Comprehension
p.12

1	C
2	A
3	D
4	B
5	D
6	C
7	D
8	B
9	B
10	D
11	B
12	A
13	A
14	D
15	B
16	C
17	D
18	A
19	C
20	D

Pictures 1
p.19

1	B
2	B
3	D
4	A
5	C
6	E
7	E
8	D
9	A
10	B
11	C
12	E
13	E
14	B
15	B
16	D
17	D
18	B
19	E
20	D

Maths 1
p.24

1	B
2	E
3	D
4	C
5	A
6	E
7	D
8	A
9	C
10	A
11	B
12	C
13	E
14	A
15	B
16	E
17	C
18	B
19	D
20	A
21	E

Maths 2
p.30

1	07
2	63
3	06
4	10
5	05
6	67
7	80
8	24
9	17
10	30
11	07
12	15

Extended answers
for Mixed Assessment Practice Paper A

Synonyms p.7

1	C	Both words mean 'to reveal'.
2	A	Both words mean 'charming'.
3	E	Both words mean 'lacking skill or dexterity'.
4	B	Both words mean 'to go faster, to accelerate'.
5	E	Both words mean 'to avoid waste or extravagance'.
6	D	Both words mean 'brave'.
7	E	Both words mean 'having no limit'.
8	E	Both words mean 'to make a small amendment or change'.
9	A	Both words mean 'a type of behaviour that is regularly followed'.
10	C	Both words mean 'fixed, unwavering'.
11	D	Both words mean 'a difference of opinion'.
12	C	Both words mean 'to deceive'.
13	D	Both words mean 'a portion'.
14	C	Both words mean 'to recreate'.
15	C	Both words mean 'to change'.
16	D	Both words mean 'having certain skills'.
17	B	Both words mean 'to put in danger'.
18	C	Both words mean 'to be sorry for having done something wrong'.
19	E	Both words mean 'a final ending or conclusion'.
20	A	Both words mean 'true to one's word or promise'.
21	B	Both words mean 'to make known'.
22	C	Both words mean 'excellent or desirable; most suitable'.
23	D	Both words mean 'showing good manners'.
24	B	Both words mean 'to make longer'.
25	B	Both words mean 'a quick look'.
26	D	Both words mean 'to become visible; to give an impression of having a certain quality'.
27	E	Both words mean 'to shout or scoff at someone unkindly'.

Comprehension p.12

1	C	A is true as lines 32 and 33 state 'he was considered to be an important figure in the Civil Rights Movement'. B is true as lines 12 and 13 state 'He was the first black recording artist to have ultimate control over his business affairs.' C is not true as lines 2 and 3 state 'he contributed to the rise of legendary singers Aretha Franklin and Marvin Gaye'. D is true as lines 15–19 talk about Cooke's stance on racism.
2	A	Line 23 states 'Cooke married his first wife, Dolores, in 1953 and they divorced five years later.' Lines 25–25 state 'In the same year as his divorce, he married his second wife, Barbara.'
3	D	The word 'poignant' means 'strong in mental appeal' or 'touching'.
4	B	Line 27 states 'On 11 December 1964, Cooke was gunned down and killed in a Californian motel.'
5	D	Lines 21 and 22 state 'had it not been somewhat overshadowed by The Beatles' high-profile appearance on an American television show around the same time.'
6	C	Line 13 states 'Cooke achieved around 30 Top 40 chart hits'.
7	D	Line 9 states '…and recording a mix of soul, and rhythm and blues'.
8	B	Line 1 states 'Sam Cooke was born on 22 January 1931'. Line 27 states 'On 11 December 1964, Cooke was gunned down…'.
9	B	Lines 37 and 38 describe how the audience were to be separated.
10	D	Lines 15–17 state 'In 1963, Cooke was moved upon hearing Bob Dylan's 'Blowin' in the Wind' and, ashamed that he hadn't written such a poignant anti-racism song himself, he embarked on the task of penning his own.'
11	B	The word 'prolific' has the same meaning as 'productive'.
12	A	Line 8 states 'but he added the 'e' to signify a fresh start'.
13	A	Line 18 states 'Cooke released 'A Change is Gonna Come' in 1964' and line 27 states 'On 11 December 1964, Cooke was gunned down and killed…'.
14	D	Line 38 states 'only one side of three balconies had been reserved for black audience members'.
15	B	Line 31 states she 'highlights the fact that his injuries did not coincide with Franklin's description…'.
16	C	Line 5 states he 'began singing, when aged six, in a group alongside his siblings'.
17	D	Lines 42–43 state 'This sense of integrity meant that his was one of the first real efforts in civil disobedience that would send a message of protest in aid of the Civil Rights Movement.'
18	A	Line 9 states 'Unhappy with his deal with RCA Records…'.
19	C	Line 20 states 'This song quickly became an anthem of the Civil Rights Movement…'.
20	D	There is no mention of Martin Luther King Jr in the text.

Pictures 1 p.19

1	B	From left to right, the stripes in the circle have reversed; eliminate C and E. The shading in the inner shapes is reversed; eliminate A and D.
2	B	From left to right, the picture comprises all the smaller shapes.
3	D	From left to right, the top shape increases in size; eliminate A and C. The bottom shape increases in size; eliminate E. The background shape becomes the foreground shape and vice versa; eliminate B.
4	A	From left to right, the picture is deconstructed from 3D to its net.
5	C	From left to right, the inner shape becomes the outer shape; the outer shape becomes the inner shape and is inverted.
6	E	From left to right, the picture is rotated 90 degrees anticlockwise.
7	E	From left to right, the number of circles remains at four. The number of sides in the shape is doubled.
8	D	From left to right, the picture is reflected.
9	A	From left to right, the shading is reversed; the solid inner lines of the star are removed and the star shape outlined by the thin dotted line becomes shaded, and vice versa.
10	B	From left to right, the shading in the outer segment becomes the shading of the inner segment and the subsequent shading also moves on by one each time.
11	C	From left to right, the shape has been turned 180 degrees. The length of lines with shapes on the end have been inverted.
12	E	From left to right, the smaller shapes have the shading reversed.
13	E	From left to right, the shape rotates 45 degrees clockwise and the distance between the lines is increased.
14	B	From top to bottom, the picture is reflected vertically and the shading transposed.
15	B	From left to right, the picture has been rotated 90 degrees clockwise.
16	D	From left to right, the shapes are flipped vertically and the lines move to the opposite position.
17	D	The shapes changes from black/white. The shapes do not rotate and keep their positions. The angle of the lines change by around 45 degrees and the distance between the lines is decreased.
18	B	From left to right, the pictures are reflected.
19	E	From left to right, the picture is rotated 90 degrees anticlockwise. The order of shapes from background to foreground has been reversed.
20	D	From left to right, the pictures are reflected.

Extended answers
for Mixed Assessment Practice Paper A

Maths 1 p.24

1	B	There are 24 hours in a day ($\frac{14}{24}$), which, when simplified, is equivalent to $\frac{7}{12}$.
2	E	This question is asking what is the lowest common multiple of 3, 4 and 5. The answer is 60.
3	D	1 hour and 5 minutes – a quarter of an hour (15 minutes) = 50 minutes 10:05am + 50 minutes = 10:55am
4	C	$13 \times 13 = 169$. Therefore the square root of 169 is 13.
5	A	$13 \times 12 = 156$
6	E	The pattern increases by 1.5km per month. July will equal 7.5km. Therefore, August will be 9km.
7	D	$\frac{24}{60}$ is equal to 0.4 or 40%.
8	A	The children's tickets will cost £760.00 – (£760.00 ÷ 4) = £570.00 each. Therefore, the total cost will be £760.00 + £760.00 + £570.00 + £570.00 (£2660.00)
9	C	64 is both 8^2 and 4^3.
10	A	Regular polygons have exactly the same number of lines of symmetry as they have sides. An octagon has eight sides and, therefore, eight lines of symmetry.
11	B	If the price has already been reduced by one-third, £24.00 must, therefore, equal two-thirds. £12.00 must equal one-third. Three-thirds must equal £12.00 × 3 (£36.00).
12	C	$8 \times 6 + 6 = 54$ $9 \times 3 = 27$ The missing number must equal 27.
13	E	$2 + 3 + 4 = 9$ $162 \div 9 = 18$. $18 \times 4 = 72$
14	A	$73 - 7 = 66$. $66 \div 2 = 33$. $33 + 7 = 40$
15	B	The difference in the bill equals £10.50 and the difference in the orders is one Hawaiian pizza. Therefore, the cost of a pizza is £10.50.
16	E	18,422 rounded to the nearest 100 is 18,400.
17	C	£11.99 + £3.99 + £7.99 + £8.99 = £32.96. Two £20 notes equal £40.00. £40.00 – £32.96 = £7.04.
18	B	There are 9 hours between 08:00 and 17:00. This means Simon's watch will show 9 × 20 seconds before 17:00. This is 3 minutes before 17:00, which is 16:57.
19	D	If eight cereal bars cost £3.20, one cereal bar will cost £3.20 ÷ 8 (40p). 40p × 10 = £4.00
20	A	$4^2 = 16$ and $7^2 = 49$. $16 + 49 = 65$
21	E	$\frac{1}{8}$ of 300ml = 37.5. $37.5 \times 5 = 187.50$ml

Maths 2 p.30

1	07	The tables of four can accommodate a total of 16 people. Therefore, the remaining 14 customers will be accommodated on $14 \div 2 = 7$ tables.
2	63	$21 \times 6 = 126$. 50% of 126 = 63 books.
3	06	(12 netball) + (14 football) = 26. $32 - 26 = 6$
4	10	If the mean age is 27, the ages must total $27 \times 4 = 108$. $44 + 42 + 12 = 98$ $108 - 98 = 10$, so Aayon is 10 years old.
5	05	$4 \times 8 = 32$. $12 \times 4 = 48$. $48 + 32 = 80$. $100 - 80 = 20$. Therefore, Anya will need to buy five more packs of batteries ($5 \times 4 = 20$)
6	67	$180 - 1 = 179$. $179 - 45 = 134$. $134 \div 2 = 67$
7	80	$\frac{2}{9}$ of 360 = 80. Therefore 80 bananas need to be thrown away.
8	24	Priya will need 4 tiles for the width and 6 tiles for the length. $4 \times 6 = 24$
9	17	Bianca can have either 13, 14, 15, 16, 17, 18 or 19 books. If she divides 13 by 2, 1 book is left over. Dividing by 3, 1 book is left over. If she divides 14 by 2, 0 books are left over. Dividing by 3, 2 books are left over. If she divides 15 by 2, 1 book is left over. Dividing by 3, 0 books are left over. If she divides 16 by 2, 0 books are left over. Dividing by 3, 1 book is left over. If she divides 17 by 2, 1 book is left over. Dividing by 3, 2 books are left over. If she divides 18 by 2, 0 books are left over. Dividing by 3, 0 books are left over. If she divides 19 by 2, 1 book is left over. Dividing by 3, 1 book is left over. Therefore, Bianca must have 17 books.
10	30	The recipe would need to be multiplied by 5. ($4000ml \div 800ml = 5$) $5 \times 6 = 30$ pineapples
11	07	$525 \div 75 = 7$
12	15	20 in a ratio of 1:3 is equal to 5:15.

CEM-style 11+ Mixed Assessment Practice Paper B

Information about this practice paper:

- The time allowed is given at the start of each section.

- The page number appears at the bottom of each page.

- The title of each section is provided at the start of each section.

- Use the pages of the test to write your workings out.

- Answers should be clearly marked in pencil on the answer sheets on pages 64 and 65, in the spaces provided. Additional answer sheets are available at **https://shop.scholastic.co.uk/pass-your-11-plus/extras**.

- If you make a mistake, rub it out and insert your new answer.

- If you are not sure of an answer, choose the one you think would be best; do not leave it blank.

 You will see this symbol at the beginning of each section. It will tell you how many minutes are allowed for that section.

Antonyms

Instructions

Select the word that has the OPPOSITE meaning to the word on the left.
Mark your answer on the answer sheet (page 64) by choosing one of the options A to E.

There is only one right answer for each question.

Example 1

	A	B	C	D	E
minority	miserly	majority	many	majorly	youngest

The correct answer is:

B

majority

The answer, B, has been marked for you on the answer sheet.

Example 2

	A	B	C	D	E
arrive	late	hurry	depart	travel	stay

The correct answer is:

C

depart

Mark the box with the letter C on the answer sheet.

 ## You have **6** minutes for this section.

1

calm

A	B	C	D	E
tolerant	transient	transparent	triumphant	turbulent

2

true

A	B	C	D	E
infamous	fractious	fictitious	notorious	ambiguous

3

important

A	B	C	D	E
boring	vexing	trifling	annoying	riveting

4

composed

A	B	C	D	E
faulty	frivolous	fluttered	flattered	flustered

5

centre

A	B	C	D	E
outlets	outcomes	outfits	outskirts	outcasts

6

fortunate

A	B	C	D	E
unable	uncanny	unlucky	unhappy	unspoilt

7

encourage

A	B	C	D	E
promote	deter	prolong	ponder	divert

8 | | A | B | C | D | E |
|---|---|---|---|---|---|
| **waste** | squander | conserve | manage | exhaust | lavish |

9 | | A | B | C | D | E |
|---|---|---|---|---|---|
| **obscure** | ominous | oblivious | obnoxious | obvious | onerous |

10 | | A | B | C | D | E |
|---|---|---|---|---|---|
| **formal** | occasional | accidental | gradual | manual | casual |

11 | | A | B | C | D | E |
|---|---|---|---|---|---|
| **broken** | innate | infirm | intact | inactive | injured |

12 | | A | B | C | D | E |
|---|---|---|---|---|---|
| **despairing** | tactful | harmful | dutiful | hurtful | hopeful |

13 | | A | B | C | D | E |
|---|---|---|---|---|---|
| **dirty** | listless | useless | flawless | spotless | pointless |

14 | | A | B | C | D | E |
|---|---|---|---|---|---|
| **provoke** | worry | torment | perturb | pacify | prevent |

15

improve

A	B	C	D	E
deteriorate	collaborate	invigorate	dominate	eradicate

16

fake

A	B	C	D	E
aromatic	emphatic	automatic	erratic	authentic

17

notice

A	B	C	D	E
flip	score	hit	throw	miss

18

publicity

A	B	C	D	E
confidence	refuge	privacy	security	mystery

19

attractive

A	B	C	D	E
inclusive	repulsive	excessive	intrusive	defensive

20

ally

A	B	C	D	E
competitor	contestant	player	candidate	opponent

21

plain

A	B	C	D	E
orderly	moderate	alternate	ornate	opaque

22	A	B	C	D	E
outside	interior	inferior	ulterior	exterior	superior

23	A	B	C	D	E
illuminate	darken	deepen	outline	erase	stifle

24	A	B	C	D	E
honesty	disgust	dialogue	deceit	disgrace	decency

25	A	B	C	D	E
remove	pinch	press	primp	pause	place

26	A	B	C	D	E
incapable	plentiful	thoughtful	skilful	neglectful	graceful

Maths 3

Instructions

In this section you will be asked to mark your answers on the answer sheet (page 64) by choosing one of the options A to J shown at the top of each page.

A	B	C	D	E	F	G	H	I	J
72	75	56	60	28	52	26	48	80	90

Example 1

What is 14 + 38?

The answer is

F
52

The answer, F, has been marked for you on the answer sheet.

Example 2

What is 194 − 168?

The answer is

G
26

Mark the box with the letter G on the answer sheet.

 You have 15 minutes for this section.

A	B	C	D	E	F	G	H	I	J
£2.10	£36.00	£3.75	£4.55	£5.20	£12.00	£14.00	£5.45	£6.10	£4.90

1 Annie visits a coffee shop and buys two croissants at £1.75 each.

She also buys a hot chocolate with marshmallows and cream which costs £1.95.

How much change should Annie receive from a £10 note?

2 Mateo notices that flowers are reduced by 30% at his corner shop.

He chooses a bunch that were originally priced at £7.00.

How much do the flowers cost after the discount?

3 Seamus is going to share £48.00 between his two daughters in the ratio 6:2.

His eldest daughter is to receive the larger amount.

How much will the smaller amount of money be?

4 Three identical notebooks cost a total of £15.60.

What is the price of one notebook?

A	B	C	D	E	F	G	H	I	J
21.00	23.00	14.00	17.00	08.00	06.00	02.00	04.00	10.00	12.00

5 Jake boards a nine-hour flight from Tokyo to Paris at 19:00 local time.

The time in Japan is five hours ahead of France.

What will the time be in Paris when the plane lands?

---

6 Zahra catches a 14:00 flight from New York to London that takes seven hours to complete its journey.

If London is five hours ahead of New York, what will the time be in London when the plane touches down?

---

7 Matt flies from Singapore to Sydney on a three-hour flight.

Sydney is three hours ahead of Singapore and his plane lands safely on time at 14:00 local time.

At what time did Matt take off from Singapore?

---

8 Ruby boards a 12-hour flight from London to Shanghai at 19:00 local time.

The time in Shanghai is seven hours ahead of London.

What will the local time be in Shanghai when the plane lands?

A	B	C	D	E	F	G	H	I	J
50	140	10	350	12	200	20	400	40	440

Euros	Indian rupees	Australian dollars
1.40	90	2

The table above shows the exchange rates for foreign currency at the bank.
Each of the above currencies is equal to 1 British pound.

9 Saanvi has 1800 Indian rupees.

How many British pounds would she be able to exchange this for at the bank?

10 Scott has £25 which he wishes to exchange for Australian dollars.

How many Australian dollars could Scott get for £25?

11 The Campbell family have returned from their holiday in Portugal.

They have brought back 560 euros which they wish to exchange for British pounds.

How many British pounds will they receive for their euros?

A	B	C	D	E	F	G	H	I	J
4 hours	3 hours	1 hour	2 hours	12 hours	5 hours	6 hours	36 hours	7 hours	24 hours

Year 5 timetable

	Monday	Tuesday	Wednesday	Thursday	Friday
09.00–09.15	Assembly	Assembly	Assembly	Assembly	Assembly
09.15–10.15	Maths	Maths	Geography	Maths	Music
10.15–10.30	Break	Break	Break	Break	Break
10.30–11.30	English	English	English	PE	English
11.30–12.30	PE	IT	Drama	IT	Maths
12.30–13.15	Lunch	Lunch	Lunch	Lunch	Lunch
13.15–14.15	English	Art	Maths	English	RE
14.15–14.30	Break	Break	Break	Break	Break
14.30–15.30	Science	History	DT	RE	Music

Information: one term = 12 weeks

12 How many hours each week are spent on maths?

_____

13 How much longer each week is spent on English than maths?

_____

14 How long in total do Year 5 spend having IT and DT lessons each week?

_____

15 How many hours do Year 5 spend on drama lessons each term?

_____

16 How many hours in total do Year 5 spend on PE during one term?

A	B	C	D	E	F	G	H	I	J
72mph	80mph	66mph	60mph	10mph	15mph	75mph	48mph	12mph	45mph

17 What is the average speed of a coach leaving Bristol at 07:30 in the morning and arriving at Swindon, 40 miles away, at 08.10?

_____

18 Maya drove her taxi from Edinburgh to Glasgow.

The journey was over a distance of 44 miles.

Maya completed the trip in 55 minutes.

What was her average speed?

_____

19 Ravi cycles to school every Monday and Friday.

He leaves home at 08.10 and it takes him 20 minutes to complete his four-mile journey.

What is Ravi's average speed?

_____

20 Hazel buys a new sports car and drives it from Land's End to John o' Groats.

The journey takes exactly 12 hours.

The total distance is 864 miles.

What was Hazel's average speed in mph?

Instructions

Look at the sequence of pictures on the left.
Two pictures are missing and are shown by a question mark.
Pick two pictures from A to F on the right that best complete the sequence.
Mark your answers on the answer sheet (page 65) by choosing from the options A to F.

Examples 1 and 2

The answer to example 1 is D.

The answer, D, has been marked for you on the answer sheet.

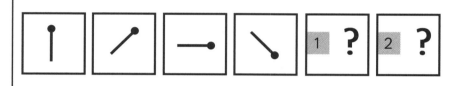

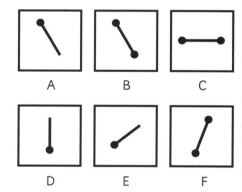

The answer to example 2 is E.

Mark the correct answer, E, on the answer sheet.

 You have 11 minutes for this section.

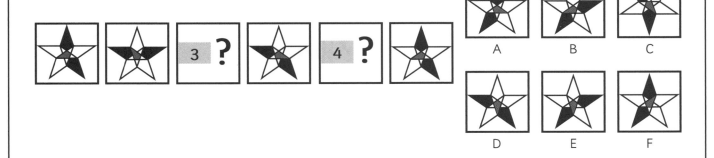

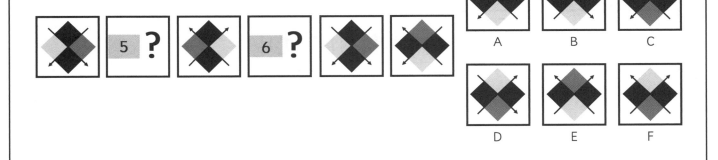

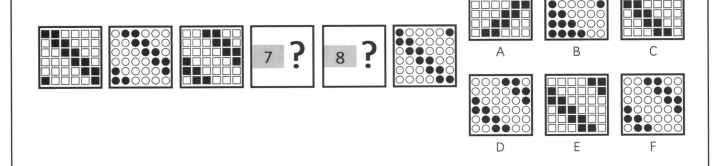

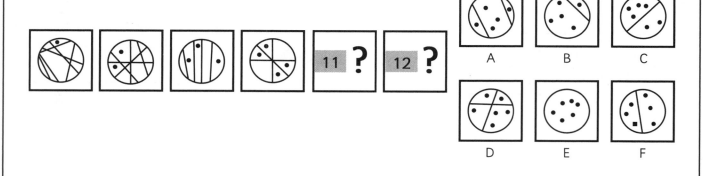

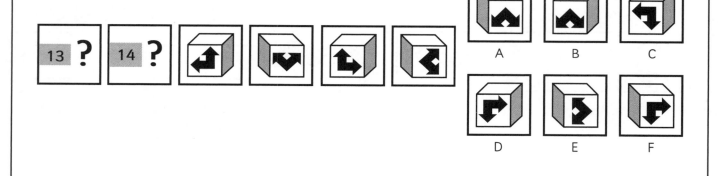

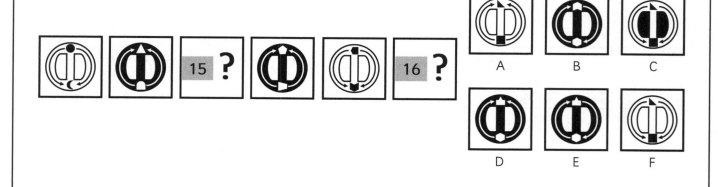

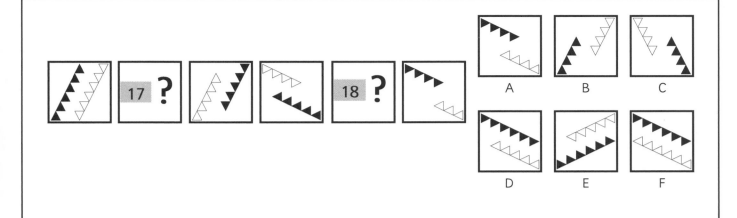

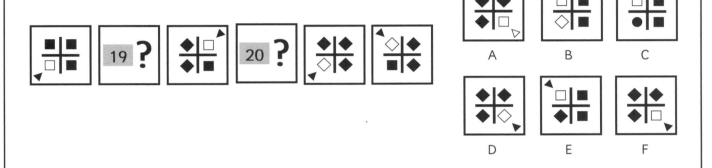

Cloze

Instructions

In the following passages, some of the words are missing. Please complete each passage by selecting the words from the options A to J. For each question, choose one word from A to J and mark this on the answer sheet (page 65).

Each word can only be used once.

Example passage

A	B	C	D	E	F	G	H	I	J
madly	crown	peace	truly	strong	sturdy	people	divided	petite	waste

For 45 years from 1558 to 1603, a (Example 1) remarkable woman governed England. By force of personality and political skill, Queen Elizabeth I united her (Example 2) country and presided over a glorious period in the arts and culture.

Example 1

The answer to the example is D as the sentence should read:
For 45 years from 1558 to 1603, a truly remarkable woman governed England.

The answer, D, has been marked for you on the answer sheet.

Example 2

The answer to example 2 is H, as the sentence should read:
By force of personality and political skill, Queen Elizabeth I united her divided country and presided over a glorious period in the arts and culture.

Mark the box with the letter H on the answer sheet.

 You have **7** minutes for this section.

Passage 1

A	B	C	D	E	F	G	H	I	J
groom	defend	doctor	itchy	after	sought	grew	evolved	patchy	medical

Scientists believe that bees first (Question **1**) around 100 million years ago, during the Cretaceous period. Bees are vegetarian, eating pollen and nectar from plants, and flying from flower to flower in search of food.

Most species of bee have stingers, which they can use to (Question **2**) themselves if they feel threatened. If you've ever been stung by a bee, then you'll already know that a bee sting can be quite painful, but isn't really that serious. The skin may swell up and be a little (Question **3**) for a couple of days, but a single bee sting usually doesn't require a trip to the doctor. However, a small number of people are allergic to bee stings. For them, a bee sting can cause a very serious reaction, such as dizziness or difficulty breathing. For this small group of people, urgent (Question **4**) attention should be (Question **5**).

Passage 2

A	B	C	D	E	F	G	H	I	J
highly	stung	rest	wings	tasks	guests	attack	move	role	flies

Some types of bee, such as the honeybee, can only sting an enemy once. This is because the stinger gets stuck in their enemy's skin, and gets pulled apart from the (Question **6**) of the bee's body when it flies away. This means the bee dies after it stings you. Other types of bee, such as bumblebees, don't lose their stinger after they (Question **7**). This means that, just like wasps, they can sting you as many times as they like.

Honeybees live in giant, (Question **8**) organised colonies that are made up of over 60,000 individual bees. A honeybee colony is made up of different types of bee, each playing an indispensable (Question **9**) within the hive. Worker bees are female, and are responsible for a large number of (Question **10**) throughout their short lives. They take care of the queen, help to feed young bees that have recently hatched, and guard the hive entrance to protect it from invaders.

Passage 3

A	B	C	D	E	F	G	H	I	J
uses	average	relies	part	crowded	larger	sticky	source	set	establish

During the spring and summer months, worker bees also leave the hive daily to gather pollen, nectar and water, bring it back to the hive and use it to produce honey. The hive (Question **11**) on this honey as its only (Question **12**) of food during the winter, when there are no flowers in bloom.

Each colony has only one queen at any one time. The queen is about twice the size of the (Question **13**) worker bee and spends all of her time laying eggs. The queen can lay up to 1500 eggs per day, and can live for several years. If a bee colony becomes too (Question **14**), a second queen will hatch and leave the hive with about half of the worker bees to (Question **15**) a new colony elsewhere.

Passage 4

A	B	C	D	E	F	G	H	I	J
like	create	inhabiting	reside	known	built	existing	solitary	lost	nectar

Honeybees are one of the most well-(Question **16**) species of bee because we humans also like to use the honey and beeswax that honeybees produce. Their hives contain honeycomb – sheets of hexagonal cells created from beeswax.

But not all species of bee live in hives. In fact, across the world around 85% of bee species live (Question **17**) lives. They don't produce honey, and they (Question **18**) only small nests that are large enough to fit just a few eggs.

Carpenter bees, for example, build their nests out of wood and will typically (Question **19**) in a tree hollow.

Plasterer bees prefer to dig holes in the ground, while other bee species simply take advantage of (Question **20**) materials they can find in the wild, like an empty snail shell.

Shuffled sentences

Instructions

Look at the examples. All the words form a sentence with one word left over. Select the word that does NOT belong in the sentence. Choose only one word for each sentence.

Mark your answer on the answer sheet (page 65) by choosing the letter, A to H, of the correct word.

Example 1

A	B	C	D	E	F	G	H
the	by	aeroplane	delayed	was	minutes	stopped	thirty

The sentence is:

A	C	E	D	B	H	F
the	aeroplane	was	delayed	by	thirty	minutes

So the leftover word is:

G
stopped

The answer, G, has been marked for you on the answer sheet.

Example 2

A	B	C	D	E	F	G	H
able	to	trainers	Yasmine	run	very	quickly	is

The sentence is:

D	H	A	B	E	F	G
Yasmine	is	able	to	run	very	quickly

So the leftover word is:

C
trainers

Mark the box with the letter C on the answer sheet.

 You have 8 minutes for this section.

1

A	B	C	D	E	F	G	H
bought	a	car	electric	Clare	of	herself	new

2

A	B	C	D	E	F	G	H
been	she	another	for	a	waiting	while	had

3

A	B	C	D	E	F	G	H
looking	need	am	my	to	I	forward	holiday

4

A	B	C	D	E	F	G	H
a	station	there	queue	the	at	was	nearly

5

A	B	C	D	E	F	G	H
finally	of	fear	flying	top	Seth	his	conquered

6

A	B	C	D	E	F	G	H
model	an	a	Ali	out	made	clay	of

7

A	B	C	D	E	F	G	H
down	rock	jagged	Danielle	the	face	clearly	abseiled

8	A	B	C	D	E	F	G	H
	then	moved	in	years	house	we	twice	two

9	A	B	C	D	E	F	G	H
	arranged	into	order	shelves	books	Angus	his	alphabetical

10	A	B	C	D	E	F	G	H
	babies	care	constant	and	young	few	need	attention

11	A	B	C	D	E	F	G	H
	very	about	purpose	his	Jakob	achievements	modest	is

12	A	B	C	D	E	F	G	H
	dog	over	its	onto	the	rolled	back	name

13	A	B	C	D	E	F	G	H
	same	wrote	occasion	the	for	Ed	song	a

14	A	B	C	D	E	F	G	H
	had	the	wide	window	required	someone	left	open

Answer sheets

Student name:

Antonyms p.43

Examples:

| 1 | [A] | [B] | [C] | [D] | [E] |
| 2 | [A] | [B] | [C] | [D] | [E] |

Questions

1	[A]	[B]	[C]	[D]	[E]
2	[A]	[B]	[C]	[D]	[E]
3	[A]	[B]	[C]	[D]	[E]
4	[A]	[B]	[C]	[D]	[E]
5	[A]	[B]	[C]	[D]	[E]
6	[A]	[B]	[C]	[D]	[E]
7	[A]	[B]	[C]	[D]	[E]
8	[A]	[B]	[C]	[D]	[E]
9	[A]	[B]	[C]	[D]	[E]
10	[A]	[B]	[C]	[D]	[E]
11	[A]	[B]	[C]	[D]	[E]
12	[A]	[B]	[C]	[D]	[E]
13	[A]	[B]	[C]	[D]	[E]
14	[A]	[B]	[C]	[D]	[E]
15	[A]	[B]	[C]	[D]	[E]
16	[A]	[B]	[C]	[D]	[E]
17	[A]	[B]	[C]	[D]	[E]
18	[A]	[B]	[C]	[D]	[E]
19	[A]	[B]	[C]	[D]	[E]
20	[A]	[B]	[C]	[D]	[E]
21	[A]	[B]	[C]	[D]	[E]
22	[A]	[B]	[C]	[D]	[E]
23	[A]	[B]	[C]	[D]	[E]
24	[A]	[B]	[C]	[D]	[E]
25	[A]	[B]	[C]	[D]	[E]
26	[A]	[B]	[C]	[D]	[E]

Maths 3 p.48

Examples:

| 1 | [A] | [B] | [C] | [D] | [E] | [F] | [G] | [H] | [I] | [J] |
| 2 | [A] | [B] | [C] | [D] | [E] | [F] | [G] | [H] | [I] | [J] |

Questions

1	[A]	[B]	[C]	[D]	[E]	[F]	[G]	[H]	[I]	[J]
2	[A]	[B]	[C]	[D]	[E]	[F]	[G]	[H]	[I]	[J]
3	[A]	[B]	[C]	[D]	[E]	[F]	[G]	[H]	[I]	[J]
4	[A]	[B]	[C]	[D]	[E]	[F]	[G]	[H]	[I]	[J]
5	[A]	[B]	[C]	[D]	[E]	[F]	[G]	[H]	[I]	[J]
6	[A]	[B]	[C]	[D]	[E]	[F]	[G]	[H]	[I]	[J]
7	[A]	[B]	[C]	[D]	[E]	[F]	[G]	[H]	[I]	[J]
8	[A]	[B]	[C]	[D]	[E]	[F]	[G]	[H]	[I]	[J]
9	[A]	[B]	[C]	[D]	[E]	[F]	[G]	[H]	[I]	[J]
10	[A]	[B]	[C]	[D]	[E]	[F]	[G]	[H]	[I]	[J]
11	[A]	[B]	[C]	[D]	[E]	[F]	[G]	[H]	[I]	[J]
12	[A]	[B]	[C]	[D]	[E]	[F]	[G]	[H]	[I]	[J]
13	[A]	[B]	[C]	[D]	[E]	[F]	[G]	[H]	[I]	[J]
14	[A]	[B]	[C]	[D]	[E]	[F]	[G]	[H]	[I]	[J]
15	[A]	[B]	[C]	[D]	[E]	[F]	[G]	[H]	[I]	[J]
16	[A]	[B]	[C]	[D]	[E]	[F]	[G]	[H]	[I]	[J]
17	[A]	[B]	[C]	[D]	[E]	[F]	[G]	[H]	[I]	[J]
18	[A]	[B]	[C]	[D]	[E]	[F]	[G]	[H]	[I]	[J]
19	[A]	[B]	[C]	[D]	[E]	[F]	[G]	[H]	[I]	[J]
20	[A]	[B]	[C]	[D]	[E]	[F]	[G]	[H]	[I]	[J]

Pictures 2 p.54

Examples:

1	[A]	[B]	[C]	~~[D]~~	[E]	[F]
2	[A]	[B]	[C]	[D]	[E]	[F]

Questions

1	[A]	[B]	[C]	[D]	[E]	[F]
2	[A]	[B]	[C]	[D]	[E]	[F]
3	[A]	[B]	[C]	[D]	[E]	[F]
4	[A]	[B]	[C]	[D]	[E]	[F]
5	[A]	[B]	[C]	[D]	[E]	[F]
6	[A]	[B]	[C]	[D]	[E]	[F]
7	[A]	[B]	[C]	[D]	[E]	[F]
8	[A]	[B]	[C]	[D]	[E]	[F]
9	[A]	[B]	[C]	[D]	[E]	[F]
10	[A]	[B]	[C]	[D]	[E]	[F]
11	[A]	[B]	[C]	[D]	[E]	[F]
12	[A]	[B]	[C]	[D]	[E]	[F]
13	[A]	[B]	[C]	[D]	[E]	[F]
14	[A]	[B]	[C]	[D]	[E]	[F]
15	[A]	[B]	[C]	[D]	[E]	[F]
16	[A]	[B]	[C]	[D]	[E]	[F]
17	[A]	[B]	[C]	[D]	[E]	[F]
18	[A]	[B]	[C]	[D]	[E]	[F]
19	[A]	[B]	[C]	[D]	[E]	[F]
20	[A]	[B]	[C]	[D]	[E]	[F]

Cloze p.58

Examples:

1	[A]	[B]	[C]	~~[D]~~	[E]	[F]	[G]	[H]	[I]	[J]
2	[A]	[B]	[C]	[D]	[E]	[F]	[G]	[H]	[I]	[J]

Questions

1	[A]	[B]	[C]	[D]	[E]	[F]	[G]	[H]	[I]	[J]
2	[A]	[B]	[C]	[D]	[E]	[F]	[G]	[H]	[I]	[J]
3	[A]	[B]	[C]	[D]	[E]	[F]	[G]	[H]	[I]	[J]
4	[A]	[B]	[C]	[D]	[E]	[F]	[G]	[H]	[I]	[J]
5	[A]	[B]	[C]	[D]	[E]	[F]	[G]	[H]	[I]	[J]
6	[A]	[B]	[C]	[D]	[E]	[F]	[G]	[H]	[I]	[J]
7	[A]	[B]	[C]	[D]	[E]	[F]	[G]	[H]	[I]	[J]
8	[A]	[B]	[C]	[D]	[E]	[F]	[G]	[H]	[I]	[J]
9	[A]	[B]	[C]	[D]	[E]	[F]	[G]	[H]	[I]	[J]
10	[A]	[B]	[C]	[D]	[E]	[F]	[G]	[H]	[I]	[J]
11	[A]	[B]	[C]	[D]	[E]	[F]	[G]	[H]	[I]	[J]
12	[A]	[B]	[C]	[D]	[E]	[F]	[G]	[H]	[I]	[J]
13	[A]	[B]	[C]	[D]	[E]	[F]	[G]	[H]	[I]	[J]
14	[A]	[B]	[C]	[D]	[E]	[F]	[G]	[H]	[I]	[J]
15	[A]	[B]	[C]	[D]	[E]	[F]	[G]	[H]	[I]	[J]
16	[A]	[B]	[C]	[D]	[E]	[F]	[G]	[H]	[I]	[J]
17	[A]	[B]	[C]	[D]	[E]	[F]	[G]	[H]	[I]	[J]
18	[A]	[B]	[C]	[D]	[E]	[F]	[G]	[H]	[I]	[J]
19	[A]	[B]	[C]	[D]	[E]	[F]	[G]	[H]	[I]	[J]
20	[A]	[B]	[C]	[D]	[E]	[F]	[G]	[H]	[I]	[J]

Shuffled sentences p.61

Examples:

1	[A]	[B]	[C]	[D]	[E]	[F]	~~[G]~~	[H]
2	[A]	[B]	[C]	[D]	[E]	[F]	[G]	[H]

Questions

1	[A]	[B]	[C]	[D]	[E]	[F]	[G]	[H]
2	[A]	[B]	[C]	[D]	[E]	[F]	[G]	[H]
3	[A]	[B]	[C]	[D]	[E]	[F]	[G]	[H]
4	[A]	[B]	[C]	[D]	[E]	[F]	[G]	[H]
5	[A]	[B]	[C]	[D]	[E]	[F]	[G]	[H]
6	[A]	[B]	[C]	[D]	[E]	[F]	[G]	[H]
7	[A]	[B]	[C]	[D]	[E]	[F]	[G]	[H]
8	[A]	[B]	[C]	[D]	[E]	[F]	[G]	[H]
9	[A]	[B]	[C]	[D]	[E]	[F]	[G]	[H]
10	[A]	[B]	[C]	[D]	[E]	[F]	[G]	[H]
11	[A]	[B]	[C]	[D]	[E]	[F]	[G]	[H]
12	[A]	[B]	[C]	[D]	[E]	[F]	[G]	[H]
13	[A]	[B]	[C]	[D]	[E]	[F]	[G]	[H]
14	[A]	[B]	[C]	[D]	[E]	[F]	[G]	[H]

Answers

Antonyms
p.43

1	E
2	C
3	C
4	E
5	D
6	C
7	B
8	B
9	D
10	E
11	C
12	E
13	D
14	D
15	A
16	E
17	E
18	C
19	B
20	E
21	D
22	A
23	A
24	C
25	E
26	C

Maths 3
p.48

1	D
2	J
3	F
4	E
5	B
6	G
7	E
8	C
9	G
10	A
11	H
12	F
13	C
14	B
15	E
16	J
17	D
18	H
19	I
20	A

Pictures 2
p.54

1	D
2	C
3	F
4	E
5	A
6	D
7	D
8	E
9	B
10	A
11	A
12	C
13	C
14	E
15	F
16	D
17	D
18	B
19	E
20	F

Cloze
p.58

1	H
2	B
3	D
4	J
5	F
6	C
7	G
8	A
9	I
10	E
11	C
12	H
13	B
14	E
15	J
16	E
17	H
18	B
19	D
20	G

Shuffled sentences p.61

1	F
2	C
3	B
4	H
5	E
6	B
7	G
8	A
9	D
10	F
11	C
12	H
13	A
14	E

Extended answers
for Mixed Assessment Practice Paper B

Antonyms p.43

1	E	The word 'calm' means 'peaceful', therefore the antonym would be 'turbulent'.
2	C	The word 'true' means 'correct', therefore the antonym would be 'false or fictitious'.
3	C	The word 'important' means 'not trivial', therefore the antonym would be 'trifling'.
4	E	The word 'composed' means 'calm; under control', therefore the antonym would be 'flustered'.
5	D	The word 'centre' means 'in the middle', therefore the antonym would be 'outskirts'.
6	C	The word 'fortunate' mean 'lucky', therefore the antonym would be 'unlucky'.
7	B	The word 'encourage' means 'persuade; coax', therefore the antonym would be 'deter'.
8	A	The word 'waste' means 'using something carelessly', therefore the antonym would be 'conserve'.
9	D	The word 'obscure' means 'unclear; concealed', therefore the antonym would be 'obvious'.
10	E	The word 'formal' means 'smart', therefore the antonym would be 'casual'.
11	C	The word 'broken' means 'damaged', therefore the antonym would be 'intact'.
12	E	The word 'despairing' means 'having no hope', therefore the antonym would be 'hopeful'.
13	D	The word 'dirty' means 'stained', therefore the antonym would be 'spotless'.
14	D	The word 'provoke' means 'make angry', therefore the antonym would be 'pacify'.
15	A	The word 'improve' means 'to get better', therefore the antonym would be 'deteriorate'.
16	E	The word 'fake' means 'not genuine', therefore the antonym would be 'authentic'.
17	E	The word 'notice' means 'to spot something', therefore the antonym would be 'miss'.
18	C	The word 'publicity' means 'information made known to the public', therefore the antonym would be 'privacy'.
19	B	The word 'attractive' means 'looking good', therefore the antonym would be 'repulsive'.
20	E	The word 'ally' means 'friend', therefore the antonym would be 'opponent'.
21	D	The word 'plain' means 'not decorated', therefore the antonym would be 'ornate'.
22	A	The word 'outside' means 'exterior', therefore the antonym would be 'interior'.
23	A	The word 'illuminate' means 'to light up', therefore the antonym would be 'darken'.
24	C	The word 'honesty' means 'freedom from deceit', therefore the antonym would be 'deceit'.
25	E	The word 'remove' means 'to take something out', therefore the antonym would be 'place'.
26	C	The word 'incapable' means 'unable to do something', therefore the antonym would be 'skilful'.

Extended answers
for Mixed Assessment Practice Paper B

Maths 3 p.48

1	D	£1.75 × 2 = £3.50. £3.50 + £1.95 = £5.45. £10.00 – £5.45 = £4.55
2	J	30% of £7.00 = £2.10. £7.00 – £2.10 = £4.90
3	F	£48.00 shared at a ratio of 6:2 = £36.00 and £12.00. The smaller amount is £12.00.
4	E	£15.60 ÷ 3 = £5.20
5	B	19:00 + 9 hours = 04:00. 04:00 – 5 hours = 23:00
6	G	14:00 + 7 hours = 21:00. 21:00 + 5 hours = 02:00 (the next day)
7	E	14:00 – (3 hours + 3 hours) = 08:00
8	C	19:00 + 12 hours = 07:00. 07:00 + 7 hours = 14:00
9	G	1800 ÷ 90 = 20
10	A	£25 × 2 = 50
11	H	560 ÷ 1.4 = 400
12	F	There is one hour of maths each day, so 5 hours in a week.
13	C	English = (1 hour each day + 1 hour extra on Mondays) 6 hours – 5 hours = 1 hour
14	B	ICT = (1 hour Tuesday + 1 hour Thursday) 2 hours. DT = 1 hour on Wednesdays. 2 hours + 1 hour = 3 hours
15	E	Drama = 1 hour on Wednesday. 1 term = 12 weeks (1 × 12 = 12)
16	J	PE = 1 hour Monday and 1 hour on Thursday. 2 × 12 = 24 hours
17	D	The total journey = 40 minutes. 40 miles in 40 minutes = 1 mile per minute, which is 60mph.
18	H	If Maya covered 44 miles in 55 minutes, she would have travelled 4 miles in 5 minutes. (5 minutes × 12 = 60 minutes) Therefore, her speed would have been (4 × 12) = 48mph.
19	I	If Ravi travels 4 miles in 20 minutes, he will be travelling at (4 × 3) = 12mph.
20	A	864 ÷ 12 = 72mph

Pictures 2 p.54

1 & 2	D & C	The clocks are advancing by 75 minutes in each picture.
3 & 4	F & E	In each picture, every point rotates anticlockwise into the position of the next point. The shaded section at the centre rotates clockwise each time.
5 & 6	A & D	The black squares alternate between vertical and horizontal with each picture. The shaded squares move one position anticlockwise each time. The arrows rotate 90 degrees clockwise.
7 & 8	D & E	The pictures alternate between containing squares and circles. In each picture, the number of shaded shapes at the bottom left increases by two, and the number of shaded shapes in the rest of the picture decreases by two.
9 & 10	B & A	In each picture, the crescent becomes larger and the star becomes smaller. Shadings alternate between black and white.
11 & 12	A & C	In each picture, the number of small black circles increases by one. The number of internal lines within the circles decreases by one.

Pictures 2 (cont.)

13 & 14	C & E	In each picture, the arrow rotates 45 degrees clockwise. The cube alternates between facing to the right and left.
15 & 16	F & D	In each picture, the outer shape alternates between black and white, as do the smaller shapes inside. The arrows alternate between pointing upwards and downwards.
17 & 18	D & B	In each picture, the banks of triangles rotate by 90 degrees anticlockwise and the shading is reversed. First, one of the white triangles is removed then, in the following picture, one of the black triangles is removed.
19 & 20	E & F	With each picture, one more square rotates to become a diamond shape. The triangle moves clockwise. There is only one white shape in each picture.

Cloze passage 1 p.58

Scientists believe that bees first <u>evolved</u> around 100 million years ago, during the Cretaceous period. Bees are vegetarian, eating pollen and nectar from plants, and flying from flower to flower in search of food.

Most species of bee have stingers, which they can use to <u>defend</u> themselves if they feel threatened. If you've ever been stung by a bee, then you'll already know that a bee sting can be quite painful, but isn't really that serious. The skin may swell up and be a little <u>itchy</u> for a couple of days, but a single bee sting usually doesn't require a trip to the doctor. However, a small number of people are allergic to bee stings. For them, a bee sting can cause a very serious allergic reaction, such as dizziness or difficulty breathing. For this small group of people, urgent <u>medical</u> attention should be <u>sought</u>.

Cloze passage 2 p.58

Some types of bee, such as the honeybee, can only sting an enemy once. This is because the stinger gets stuck in their enemy's skin, and gets pulled apart from the <u>rest</u> of the bee's body when it flies away. This means the bee dies after it stings you. Other types of bee, such as bumblebees, don't lose their stinger after they <u>attack</u>. This means that, just like wasps, they can sting you as many times as they like.

Honeybees live in giant, <u>highly</u> organised colonies that are made up of over 60,000 individual bees. A honeybee colony is made up of different types of bee, each playing an indispensable <u>role</u> within the hive. Worker bees are female, and are responsible for a large number of <u>tasks</u> throughout their short lives. They take care of the queen, help to feed young bees that have recently hatched, and guard the hive entrance to protect it from invaders.

Cloze passage 3 p.58

During the spring and summer months, worker bees also leave the hive daily to gather pollen, nectar and water, bring it back to the hive and use it to produce honey. The hive <u>relies</u> on this honey as its only <u>source</u> of food during the winter, when there are no flowers in bloom.

Each colony has only one queen at any one time. The queen is about twice the size of the <u>average</u> worker bee and spends all of her time laying eggs. The queen can lay up to 1500 eggs per day, and can live for several years. If a bee colony becomes too <u>crowded</u>, a second queen will hatch and leave the hive with about half of the worker bees to <u>establish</u> a new colony elsewhere.

Cloze passage 4 p.58

Honeybees are one of the most well-<u>known</u> species of bee because we humans also like to use the honey and beeswax that honeybees produce. Their hives contain honeycomb – sheets of hexagonal cells created from beeswax.

But not all species of bee live in hives. In fact, across the world around 85% of bee species live <u>solitary</u> lives. They don't produce honey, and they <u>create</u> only small nests that are large enough to fit just a few eggs.

Carpenter bees, for example, build their nests out of wood and will typically <u>reside</u> in a tree hollow.

Plasterer bees prefer to dig holes in the ground, while other bee species simply take advantage of <u>existing</u> materials they can find in the wild, like an empty snail shell.

Shuffled sentences p.61

1	F	Clare bought herself a new electric car
2	C	she had been waiting for a while
3	B	I am looking forward to my holiday
4	H	there was a queue at the station
5	E	Seth finally conquered his fear of flying
6	B	Ali made a model out of clay
7	G	Danielle abseiled down the jagged rock face
8	A	we moved house twice in two years
9	D	Angus arranged his books into alphabetical order
10	F	young babies need constant care and attention
11	C	Jakob is very modest about his achievements
12	H	the dog rolled over onto its back
13	A	Ed wrote a song for the occasion
14	E	someone had left the window wide open

Blank page